T0069959

AMANDA MAIER

SONATA IN B MINOR

for Flute and Piano

Arranged and Edited by Carol Wincenc
Co-edited by Bryan Wagorn

KEISER

Copyright © 2017 Lauren Keiser Music Publishing (ASCAP).
International Copyright Secured. All Rights Reserved.

Sonata in B Minor

for

Flute and Piano

I.

AMANDA MAIER

edited by Carol Wincenc and Bryan Wagorn

Copyright © 2017 by Lauren Keiser Music Publishing
International Copyright Secured.
All rights reserved.

Digital and photographic copying of this page is illegal.

Digital and photographic copying of this page is illegal.

Digital and photographic copying of this page is illegal.

Digital and photographic copying of this page is illegal.

6

Digital and photographic copying of this page is illegal.

Digital and photographic copying of this page is illegal.

8

Digital and photographic copying of this page is illegal.

Digital and photographic copying of this page is illegal.

Digital and photographic copying of this page is illegal.

Digital and photographic copying of this page is illegal.

Digital and photographic copying of this page is illegal.

Digital and photographic copying of this page is illegal.

Digital and photographic copying of this page is illegal.

Digital and photographic copying of this page is illegal.

II.

Digital and photographic copying of this page is illegal.

Digital and photographic copying of this page is illegal.

Digital and photographic copying of this page is illegal.

Digital and photographic copying of this page is illegal.

Digital and photographic copying of this page is illegal.

21

Digital and photographic copying of this page is illegal.

III.

Digital and photographic copying of this page is illegal.

Digital and photographic copying of this page is illegal.

Digital and photographic copying of this page is illegal.

Digital and photographic copying of this page is illegal.

Digital and photographic copying of this page is illegal.

Digital and photographic copying of this page is illegal.

Digital and photographic copying of this page is illegal.

Digital and photographic copying of this page is illegal.

Digital and photographic copying of this page is illegal.

Digital and photographic copying of this page is illegal.

Digital and photographic copying of this page is illegal.

Digital and photographic copying of this page is illegal.

Digital and photographic copying of this page is illegal.

Digital and photographic copying of this page is illegal.

Digital and photographic copying of this page is illegal.